I0210656

**STRATEGY
RESEARCH
PROJECT**

The views expressed in this paper are those of the author and do not necessarily reflect the views of the Department of Defense or any of its agencies. This document may not be released for open publication until it has been cleared by the appropriate military service or government agency.

INFLUENCE OF NAVAL POWER ON THE COURSE OF THE SPANISH CIVIL WAR, 1936-1939

BY

COMMANDER JOHN M. KERSH, Jr.
United States Navy

USAWC CLASS OF 2001

U.S. ARMY WAR COLLEGE, CARLISLE BARRACKS, PA 17013-5050

20010430 134

USAWC STRATEGY RESEARCH PROJECT

INFLUENCE OF NAVAL POWER ON THE COURSE OF THE SPANISH CIVIL WAR, 1936-1939

by

Commander John M. Kersh, Jr.
United States Navy

Colonel Brian D. Moore, USMC
Project Advisor

The views expressed in this academic research paper are those of the author and do not necessarily reflect the official policy or position of the U.S. Government, the Department of Defense, or any of its agencies.

U.S. Army War College
CARLISLE BARRACKS, PENNSYLVANIA 17013

ABSTRACT

AUTHOR: CDR John M. Kersh, Jr.

TITLE: The Influence of Naval Power on the Course of the Spanish Civil War, 1936-1939

FORMAT: Strategy Research Project

DATE: 15 March 2001   PAGES: 48   CLASSIFICATION: Unclassified

The role of the great powers in the Spanish Civil War and the war on land that they were able to influence has been much studied. What has not been studied or well understood to a great extent is the role that naval power played and its decisive influence on the war fought on the Iberian Peninsula. To appreciate how the rebels (or Nationalists) were able to overthrow a left-of center but very much democratically elected government (the Republicans) it is important to understand the role that sea power played. Spain historically has been very dependent upon imports and diligently maintained sea lines of communication with a relatively strong navy. When the government was not quickly overthrown in a coup, the coup degenerated into a war of attrition. Accordingly, each side quickly became dependent upon the importation of war materials. Should either the Republicans or Nationalists not be able to maintain their sea lines of communication, the war would be lost despite the valiant efforts of the soldiers on land. Fundamentally, the government of Spain, the Republic, lost the Spanish Civil War because they were not able to control the seas and maintain the sea lines of communication.

TABLE OF CONTENTS

THE INFLUENCE OF NAVAL POWER ON THE COURSE OF THE SPANISH CIVIL WAR, 1936-1939

THE POLITICAL SETTING OF THE SPANISH CIVIL WAR

The Spanish Civil War started July 17, 1936 and lasted until March 31, 1939. It has been one of the most studied and controversial wars of the 20th century. It was the first war to pit the unyielding ideologies of Fascism, Communism, socialism, Anarchism and the Catholic Church coupled with Spanish nationalism against one another. The explosive mix internal to Spain was further exacerbated by a variety of countries external to Spain that were attempting to resolve perceived historic balance of power inequities during the course of the war. The deeply felt emotions about the war are still held to this day by the advocates of the various ideological camps. Each history that has been written on the war has tended to be from one of the ideological perspectives. As Anthony Beevor notes, "The absolute truth about such a politically passionate subject can never be known, because nobody can discard prejudice sufficiently." It is very understandable that there is so much passion with respect to the war. For those that were involved in the war, the level of death, destruction and wanton cruelty was truly staggering. This paper will look at the participants in the Spanish Civil War from an historical perspective and attempt to deal with the war in as dispassionate a manner as possible.[1]

The role of the great powers in the Spanish Civil War and the war on land that they were able to influence has been much studied. What has not been studied or well understood to a great extent is the role that naval power played and its decisive influence on the war fought on the Iberian Peninsula. To appreciate how the rebels (or Nationalists) were able to overthrow a left-of center but very much democratically elected government (the Republicans) it is important to understand the role that sea power played. Spain historically has been very dependent upon imports (originally from colonies) and diligently maintained sea lines of communication with a relatively strong navy. When the government was not quickly overthrown in a coup, the coup degenerated into a war of attrition. Accordingly, each side quickly became dependent upon the importation of war material. Should either the Republicans or Nationalists not be able to maintain their sea lines of communication, the war would be lost despite the valiant efforts of the soldiers on land. Fundamentally, the government of Spain, the Republic, lost the war because they were not able to control the seas and maintain the sea lines of communication. Prior to discussing the influence of naval power on the course of the war, it is useful to review the historical-political events that led to the war.

The Spanish Civil War was not some simple revolt of the generals, but a conflict that embodied three distinct antagonisms that have been prevalent throughout Spanish history. The antagonisms included class interests, the tension between authoritarian rule and libertarian instincts and the role of the central government versus regionalist aspirations. The Nationalists represented the interests of the landowners and businessmen and believed in a very strong centralized authoritarian government. The Republicans believed in individual liberty but it worked against them because they were unable to sort through the competing ideologies of the socialists, Anarchists, and Communists in time to defeat the Nationalists. In contrast, the Nationalists were very much unified in their "ideology," that of the Roman Catholic Church which was the oldest and most powerful political force in Spain. The divergent ideologies that composed the Republicans had to compete against a formidable foe, the forces of traditional Spain that were inextricably linked to Catholicism. The Republicans inability to lessen the nation building aspirations of some of the regions of Spain including Basque and Catalonia further weakened their ability to confront the Nationalists effectively.[2] In the end, the Republicans would lose and the Nationalists would win at the cost of more than 600,000 lives. Some have argued that World War II for Spain started in 1936, they very well may be right.[3]

The roots of the Spanish Civil War can be traced as far back as the Reconquista of Spain from the Islamic Moors that ended in 1492 with the triumphal entry of Isabella and Ferdinand into Granada and the ejection of all the Moors from Spain. This Reconquista was a crusade sanctioned by the Pope. Those knights that fought in the reconquest took up the cross as an act of penance for the Catholic Church and to save Spain from its occupiers. Throughout the Spanish Civil War, the forces on the right (the Nationalists) would hearken back to the Reconquista and equate the fight against the forces on the left (the Republicans) as a second recovery operation against the "heathens."[4]

Spain was not politically stable in the nineteenth century because of this clash between liberalism and traditionalism. The trinity of the Army, Church, and Monarchy was all-important for keeping Spain stable politically. When the Army acted in concert with the legitimizing forces of the Church and Monarchy it could assert itself and form a relatively stable government. When the Monarchy was not perceived as legitimate (typically there was excessive corruption or Queen Isabella had "exercised her guards officers") and the government would collapse.[5]

The time between 1814-1874 was the age of the pronunciamiento. The government of Madrid was corrupt and generals would periodically overthrow the government, make a speech and declare themselves dictator. During this period there were 37 attempted coups, 12 of which were successful. The Monarchy of Queen Isabella finally collapsed in 1868 and she was deposed. She installed her lover as her successor, but he was not well received by the Army and he was deposed in 1870. In 1873 the Cortes, the Spanish Parliament, established the First Republic, but it was not to last and it too was overthrown by the military. The Army found a monarch who was perceived to be legitimate in Queen Isabella's son, Alfonso XII, who was installed by General Martinez Campos in 1874. Spain enjoyed a period of relative stability until 1923; the central government of Madrid was not overthrown despite the development of new ideologies and competing philosophies among the peoples of Spain.[6]

The Anarchists were the first ideology to take a foothold in Spain. The Anarchists were a libertarian branch of socialism that was completely incompatible with Communism. The Anarchist movement started in Spain in 1868 with the immigration of Giuseppe Fanelli. He came to Spain without being able to speak any Spanish, but he found a very receptive audience. By 1872 there were 50,000 Anarchists in Spain. The Anarchists adamantly rejected the Communist idea of the worker-state, believing that the domination of one human being by another was wrong and was the root of all evil in society. They believed that freedom and mutual aid were the foundation of society and could not begin to comprehend any other political arrangement. The federalist nature of Anarchism had great appeal—there is a historic distrust of the central government in Spain among a large portion of the population. Anarchism also had a strong moral appeal given a politically corrupt system and a Church that had aligned itself perhaps too closely with the state.[7]

Marxism also took hold in Spain during this timeframe, but it had much less appeal. The Communist emphasis on a strong central state worked against traditional Spanish distrust of the central state. The Marxists may have been able to gain a foothold in the most industrialized region of Spain, Catalonia, but the Anarchists had gotten there first. By the time of the Russian Revolution the socialists had 200,000 followers and the Anarchists had 800,000. Various workers' unions were formed that had a variety of political associations including socialist, Anarchist and various combinations of ideologies. The turmoil created during the Russian and German Revolutions combined with the harsh circumstances of the workers and peasantry in Spain and periodic imposition of martial law ensured that they were some of the most politically aware people in Europe. The mixture of ideologies was truly explosive.[8]

In September of 1923, General Primo de Rivera seized power in a preemptive coup as a result of the Spanish people's outrage at the Army. The people were angry because a division commanded by General Silvestre was ambushed in Annual, Morocco by tribesmen under Abd-el-Krim. It was a defeat for Spain on a horrific scale. Ten thousand soldiers were killed, four thousand taken prisoner and Silvestre committed suicide. General Silvestre had been encouraged to embark on a military adventure by King Alfonso who wanted a military victory to help celebrate the feast of St. James, the Army's patron saint. A formal commission investigated the loss of the division, the King was censured, but just prior to the report being released Primo de Rivera seized power. Primo was accepted by the liberal middle classes and was to last as dictator until 1930. Municipal elections were eventually held on 12 April 1931. Every large city except for Cadiz elected anti-monarchical candidates to the Spanish parliament. The King was dumbfounded at the depth of his unpopularity and abdicated on 14 April 1931. The Second Republic had arrived without resorting to violence. The Spanish thought themselves to be truly blessed and they were until the political right felt disenfranchised in 1936.[9]

In elections held in June 1931 the socialists and left-leaning Republicans were swept into power. The left-leaning government attempted to lessen the power of the Church and did not protect Church property in some instances when the property was vandalized. The government also granted home rule to the Catalonians while the Basques unsuccessfully pressed for autonomy. The traditionalists who included the Army leadership were very much offended when the Church was not adequately defended and the breakup of Spain was threatened in the government's support of regionalism. In August 1932 General Sanjurjo (who later played a key role in the war) made a pronunciamiento against the breakup of the Spanish state. The government put down the revolt easily and General Sanjurjo was forced to flee the country. When the Civil War started in 1936, the Republican leadership did not initially understand the depth of backing and the sophistication of the Nationalist generals. The Republican leadership was to a certain extent deluded into thinking this was another easily crushed revolt to the experience with General Sanjurjo.[10] As Alvarez del Vayo noted to the Soviet Ambassador to Great Britain in July 1936, "Of course, the path of the Republic is not strewn with roses, but it is not in serious danger. There are forces in the country sufficient to avert or in any event crush any attempt at a military coup."[11]

There was significant turmoil with in Spain. There was great unrest due the actions of both governmental and non-governmental forces. The labor unions were very active and there were a series of peasant uprisings. The Civil Guards were supposed to enforce order, but in a number of instances they killed innocent civilians in the course of putting down an uprising. The Civil Guards were also attacked and killed by the people. The economic situation was also tenuous and there was a large flight of capital out of the country. As a result of the turmoil, the left-leaning Republican government collapsed and elections were held 19 November 1933. The right had reorganized since the last election and they were swept into power. The left-leaning Republican government had attempted a number of reforms including redistribution of land and the increased hourly wages for workers. The new right-leaning government quickly reversed the reforms and increased the size of the Civil Guard to suppress the restless portion of the population. Things became so bad the peasants who gathered acorns to eat were arrested for stealing. In the midst of this unrest a Fascist leader, Gil Robles, demanded a majority in the ruling coalition, which the left equated to an attempt by him to takeover the government. Consequently, the left declared a preemptive labor strike to protest the actions of the Fascists on 5 October 1934. The labor strike had little effect in most of the country except for the Asturias, a mountainous mining region in Spain that had significant union influence among the workers where 50,000 workers rebelled. General Franco, who was the Chief of Staff of the Army, brutally suppressed the rebellion. Franco employed the much-feared Moorish regulares of the Army of Africa (Spanish Morocco was Franco's power base) and units of the Spanish Foreign Legion. Franco's forces quelled the revolt in an incredibly brutal manner, which, in many ways, was an initial look at how Nationalist forces would conduct themselves during the oncoming Civil War. Terror was deliberately used as a weapon. Corruption plagued the right-leaning government and it too would collapse.[12]

The left had learned their lesson when they were out of power and formed an effective coalition, called the Popular Front that included Anarchists and Communists. The Anarchists had abstained from the previous election when the right was victorious, but this time they voted. The Popular Front was swept into power in February 1936. There were immediate calls by some in the military and on the right for a coup d'etat. Franco urged caution because he was unsure as to the Civil Guards support of the left-of-center government. No coup was staged, but the political right had lost faith in the parliamentary system. The right now dedicated itself to preparing for resolving their differences with the left using non-political means. Accordingly, the nascent Fascist Falange movement grew greatly in strength.[13]

The Falange according to one of its theorists objective was "to kill the old soul of the liberal, decadent, Masonic, materialist and frenchified nineteenth century, and return to impregnate ourselves with the spirit of the imperial, heroic, sobre, Castilian, spiritual, legendary and knightly sixteenth century."[14]The ideal Falangist was perceived to be a warrior Jesuit. The Carlists were also active. The Carlists were based in the Pyrenees and they saw liberalism as the source of all evil and they wanted to revive a royal Catholic autocracy. They armed and trained a militia. Both the Falange and Carlists had ties to Mussolini in Italy and with Germany for training and weapons at this time. The Falangists and the forces on the left engaged in a series of reprisal killings during this time period.[15]

The ruling Popular Front was weak. The forces of liberal moderation were too diffuse and could not agree among themselves in a parliamentary system as to how to govern. The Communists with Comintern support eventually dominated the unions (Union General de

Trabajadores (UGT) and Confederacion Nacional de Trabajo (CNT)) and the Popular Front. The Communists also organized para-military organizations like the MAOC (Anti-Fascist Workers' and Peasants' Militia). In 1936, the Communists staged a May Day parade in Madrid that many moderates found alarming. The Falangists and the forces on the left (CNT union members) continued to conduct a series of reprisal killings.[16]

In 1933 a group of patriotic officers formed a planning committee, the Union Military Espanola, to lay the groundwork for a military coup. The government took the wise precaution of transferring the generals who could potentially stage a coup away from what was perceived to be their bases of power. Unfortunately, they sent one of the significant coup plotters, General Franco, to the Canary Islands which was not too far from Spanish Morocco and Franco's military muscle, the Army of Africa. General Mola, chief organizer of the conspiracy, was transferred to Pamplona the center of the Carlists, who promptly offered up 7000-armed militiamen.[17]

General Francisco Franco y Bahamonde played the most important role in the rebellion. Franco was born in 1892 at the naval base at El Ferrol in Galicia. Franco's father was a dissolute naval paymaster. Franco intended to be a naval officer, but there was no room at the Naval Cadet School in the aftermath of the Spanish-American War in 1898. He went instead to the Infantry Academy in Toledo in 1907. He had extensive experience in Spanish Morocco, he was the second in command of the Spanish Foreign Legion in 1920 and commanded the Spanish Foreign Legion from 1923-1927. He commanded the landing party that made the risky landing in Morocco in 1925 that led to the defeat of Abd-el-Kim. During the fight against Abd-el-Kim he showed that he was a brave officer who took calculated risks. The defeat of Abd-el-Kim made Franco a recognized hero in the Army. As a result of his suppression of the labor uprising in the Asturias in October 1934, Franco was regarded by the government as the savior of the nation. Franco was supposed to have a subordinate role in the rebellion to General Sanjurjo and then General Mola, but a series of accidents eventually eliminated both and made Franco the head of the Nationalists in June 1937.[18]

The uprising of the generals was supposed to be rapid and ruthless. The revolt was to commence at 5 am on 18 July in Spanish Morocco and then the Army of Africa was to be transported to the Andalucian coast by the Navy 24 hours later. The plan for the coup was discovered on 17 July in Melilla, Morocco and the timeline was moved up a day. The Army of Africa quickly suppressed all resistance in Spanish Morocco, but results of the uprising were mixed in Spain. The government was slow to react to the threat, thinking that the uprising was similar to the one led by Sanjurjo in 1934. Some workers were armed and some were not. The

Civil Guard would switch sides in a variety of circumstances. Those that were slow to react to the threat on the Republican side were overrun and destroyed.[19]

THE ROLE OF THE NAVY AT THE OUTSET OF THE SPANISH CIVIL WAR

The Spanish Navy played a key role at the outset of the Spanish Civil War. Franco's base of power was the Army of Africa. The Army of Africa was composed of fierce Moslem fighters and the Spanish Legion (some 32,000 men). They had significant war fighting experience and were a much more professional and competent Army than that of mainland Spain. Once resistance was suppressed in Morocco, it was most important that the Army of Africa be transported to Spain by the Spanish Navy. Senior naval officers and Franco had planned in advance that the warships were to make all speed to Spanish Morocco at the start of the uprising. It was thought that few officers would remain loyal to the government and that the ships would easily come over to the Nationalists. The officers of the Spanish Navy were aristocratic, for the most part monarchist and had little understanding of sailors who primarily had Republican sympathies. The crews were much better organized than their Army counterparts and some representatives held a secret meeting in El Ferrol, a principle naval base, on 13 July to decide what to do should the officers rebel against the government. On the morning of 18 July three destroyers were directed by the Ministry of Marine in Madrid to sail from Cartagena to Melilla and bombard an insurgent town to suppress the rebel uprising. In Madrid an enlisted telgraphist realized that the rebellion had started and promptly arrested his officer in charge who was in on the conspiracy. The enlisted telegraphist then sent a series of messages in the clear (for only the officers had code books) to the crews of the ships to inform them of what was happening. As a result, the officers did not lead the crews astray. The Minister of Marine then sent a signal to all ships dismissing all officers.[20]

On two of the three destroyers, *Almirante Valdes* and *Sanchez Barcaiztegui*, the crews overpowered their officers, elected a ship's committee and proceeded to bombard Melilla and Ceuta then returned the ships to the loyal Republican naval base of Cartagena. Only the *Churruca* remained in the officers' hands because their radio was out of order. As a result the Nationalists only had one destroyer and one gunboat, *Dato*, to ferry the Army of Africa to Spain. On the morning of the 19th the government ordered all available ships to the Strait of Gibraltar to prevent the Army of Africa from getting to Spain via ship. The crews took over ships including the cruiser *Miguel de Cervantes*, the only seaworthy battleship, the *Jaime I*, and the cruiser *Libertad*. The destroyer *Churruca* was also won back by its crew after having made one run with half a tabor (200 soldiers of the Army of Africa) of <u>regulares</u> to Cadiz.[21] Some officers resisted to the end, others quickly surrendered once the crews seized the armory. There was one famous signal exchange between the Ministry of Marine and the crew of the *Jaime Primero*. The ship sent the following signal, "Crew of *Jaime Primero* to Ministry of Marine. We have had serious resistance from the commanders and officers on board and have subdued them by force. Urgently request instructions as to bodies." Ministry of Marine to crew *Jamie Primero*. "Lower bodies overboard with respectful solemnity. What is your present position?"[22]

The enlisted crews of the Republican Navy controlled enough ships to interrupt the Nationalists' plans of transporting the Army of Africa via ship to the Spanish mainland. The Nationalists however had a back-up plan. Emissaries had been sent by Franco to meet with Adolf Hitler to secure aircraft transport for the Army of Africa. The emissaries met with Hitler on 26 July. The German Foreign Ministry and War Ministry were not interested in helping the Nationalists. They were concerned that the supply of arms to the Nationalists could not be kept secret and would result in "serious consequences for the German colonies in Spain and to German merchant and naval vessels there." They were only interested in helping the Nationalists once they were firmly in power. Admiral Canaris and General Goring acted as advocates for the Spanish emissaries and met with Adolf Hitler before representatives from the War Ministry and Foreign Ministry could make their case to Hitler. Goring noted that any aircraft that the Nationalists needed could be paid for with Spanish ore that were much needed by Germany and also that France had already decided to aid the Republican government. Hitler was convinced that the Nationalists should be helped initially in some small way and some JU-52 transport aircraft should be immediately flown to Morocco and that other aircraft and material sent by sea. As soon as the JU-52 aircraft arrived in Morocco they began shuttling the Army of Africa to Spain as quickly as possible. Franco was thus able to get approximately 1500 soldiers of the Army of Africa to Spain from July to August, but a substantial portion remained in Morocco.[23] The Nationalists needed to secure local sea control in the vicinity of the Strait of Gibraltar and get the remainder of the Army of Africa and its associated equipment to Spain.[24]

After the uprising, the Republican crews were able to secure the battleship *Jaime Primero*, three cruisers, fifteen destroyers and approximately ten submarines from Nationalist officers. The Nationalists were able to seize the naval bases El Ferrol and Cadiz, the old battleship *Espana* (in dry-dock), the modern light cruiser *Almirante Cevera*, plus the new heavy cruisers *Canaris* and *Baleares* that were under construction but near completion. The Republicans held Cartagena and all other Mediterranean ports including Malaga (located near the Strait of Gibraltar). The portion of the Navy and associated bases that the Nationalists controlled were thus quite small.[25]

The killing of the officers of the Spanish Navy had a deleterious effect on the Republic's ability to employ their preponderant naval forces against the much smaller Nationalist Navy. The former enlisted men of the Republican Navy attempted to employ the ships effectively, but they simply did not have the experience that the officers had. Some writers have noted that the Republican Navy was not able to employ their ships effectively because discipline had broken down (It was noted by British observers that prostitutes appeared to be part of ships company. "Led by the British officer to the wardroom, in which there were several flashy women of obvious profession.")[26] On-scene reports indicated that the Republican ships fought valiantly despite their lack of officers from the pre-civil war Navy. German observers were impressed with how well the Republican ships initially fought. In August of 1936 one of the German flag officers noted, "The important supply routes from Africa, the Strait of Gibraltar, and the Bay of Cadiz are completely controlled by the Red fleet. It is astonishing with what enthusiasm and effectiveness they execute their mission, especially given as there are almost no officers aboard."[27]

Unfortunately, the effectiveness of the Republican Navy was not to last. After the Republican Navy initially prevented Franco from transporting the Army of Africa via ship to Spain, it withdrew to the loyal Republican bases of Cartagena and Barcelona. It is unclear as to why the Republicans kept their ships in port vice protecting the sea lines of communication. (As will be noted in a later chapter, Russian doctrinal differences on how to employ the Republican Navy were the most likely reason that the Republican Navy was not employed effectively.) From early August onward the Nationalists were able to transport their men and supplies across the Straits of Algerciras in Gibraltar Bay almost without interruption. Of all the mistakes made by the Republican government in their attempts to suppress the rebellion, there is perhaps no greater mistake made than the failure of the Republican Navy to prevent the Army of Africa from deploying to Spain. The best soldiers of the war came from Morocco. They quickly rolled up the Republican resistance and seized large portions of Spain as they marched to Madrid. Had the Army of Africa not appeared in force in Spain the Nationalists would have been quickly crushed. The outcome of the Spanish Civil War depended as much as controlling sea lines of communication and maintaining local sea control as it did on fighting and winning battles on land.[28]

BALANCE OF POWER CONSIDERATIONS

There was great concern in the mid 1930's in Europe that another world war was close at hand. Much of Europe feared that if the war was not kept bounded that it would escalate into continental European war. The French, British, and Americans were more concerned about the war becoming a continental war than the Soviets, Germans, and Italians were. Britain, France, and the United States had more interest in Spain with respect to invested capital and markets. For Germany and France, Spain was a focal point of strategic rivalry. Both Italy and Britain were interested in Spain because it was a gateway to the Mediterranean.[29] The Germans were concerned about the recently elected French Popular Front government's overt support of the Spanish Popular Front government. Both governments had a leftist orientation and Hitler perceived that any cooperation between them would aid the spread of Communism in Europe.[30]

Britain maintained an official policy of neutrality during the war, but the British Tory leaders were not pre-disposed to shoring up the Republican/Popular Front government. Early in the war, British Prime Minster Eden told the German Charge D' Affairs, Prince Otto Von Bismarck, that the British were pro-Franco and that a victory by Nationalist forces would not weaken their maritime interests in any way. Furthermore, Britain accepted in good faith Italy's disclaimer on territorial designs in either Spain or the Balearics.[31] British interests lay in the defeat of extreme factions of both the right and left in Spain. The Admiralty was very much interested in the Communists not gaining ascendancy in Spain and, in turn, Communism not spreading from Spain to Portugal and jeopardizing Lisbon.[32] Britain was concerned that should the government in Lisbon fall, that the Portuguese colonies could possibly come under the German's purview.[33] Consequently, they acquiesced when Portugal actively helped the Nationalists. Britain was concerned about the post-war diplomatic impact should they pick the wrong side and wanted Spain to at least remain neutral with regard to British interests in the Mediterranean. They had alienated the Italians during the Italian Abyssinian campaign and did not wish to make another potential enemy in the Mediterranean.[34]

The French left-of-center government of Prime Minister Leon Blum was sympathetic to the leftist government in Spain. France was concerned about the possible expansion of the war beyond the Pyrenees, the possible interruption of sea lines of communication with their colonies in North Africa. The French did not wish to further agitate the Italians who were a threat to their Mediterranean security interests; so French policy was officially (like Great Britain) non-interventionist. Blum was embarrassed to have to depart from his ideological loyalties, but balance of power considerations predominated.[35] There was some level of cooperation between both Popular Front Governments, but the British held the level of involvement in check. The British obliquely warned that French that if they became entangled with the Spanish Popular Front government, that Britain would not come to the aid of the French in case of war. France, like Great Britain never participated in the war on an "official" basis.[36]

Germany vigorously backed up the Nationalists. The Germans wanted the Nationalists to win, but to win in such a manner that the war did not escalate into a general European war. The Germans were willing to supply the Nationalists extensively with men and material including the dispatch of the famed Condor Legion to Spain. The Germans tried to minimize the exposure of the level of their involvement whenever possible so as to have some level of deniability. The German government proclaimed an official policy of non-intervention in conflict. The French Ambassador to Germany, Andre Francois-Poncet, approached the German Foreign Minister, Baron von Neurath, on 4 August 1936 and floated the idea of a joint declaration by all interested powers regarding non-intervention in the conflict. Baron von Neurath replied that it would be superfluous for the German government to make such a statement because Germany, "naturally did not intervene in Spanish internal political affairs and disputes." The Spanish Civil War allowed Hitler to divide the British and French internally and divert their attention while he expanded territorially in Eastern Europe.[37]

Mussolini and the Italians had made two attempts in four years prior to the outbreak of the Spanish Civil War to support conspiracies to overthrow the left-of-center government of the Republic. The Italian Fascists felt kinship with the Falange and believed that the prestige of Fascism was linked to the overall success of Fascism in Spain. The Italian Fascists scorned the liberal parliamentary regime that the Republic represented and they were uneasy about the overt anti-Fascism of many in the Republican leadership. They were also concerned that the liberal democracy of the Republic would lead to Communism in Spain, and they were very concerned that Spain would draw closer to left-of-center France which would hurt Italy. The British and French had attempted to maintain cordial relations with Italy in the aftermath of the Ethiopian crisis, but Italy did not respond to their overtures. Mussolini saw the French government as a threat and wanted to recreate the Roman Empire in the Mediterranean.[38] When the war broke out in Spain, the Italians intervened decisively on behalf of the Nationalists. They, like the Germans, provided aircraft for the initial lift of a portion of the Army of Africa to Spain, later to be followed up by the massive military involvement of Italian army, air force, and naval units.[39]

The Italians were much more forthright in their involvement in the Spanish Civil War than the Germans and ran much greater risks. One example here will suffice: the Germans sent submarines U-33 and U-34 to the Mediterranean to interdict Republican shipping. The German submarine commanders had to positively identify targets prior to shooting. The submarine commanders asked for the rules of engagement to be eased, but were told, "restrictions on freedom of action are necessary so that uncovering of camouflage or mistakes do not increase the difficulties of present situation." More importantly, deception was "of the highest principle to avoid compromising Germany." The submarines left after just one patrol because it was too risky. (U-34 did sink the Republican submarine C-3 while departing the Mediterranean. No one found out about the sinking until well after the war).[40] The Italians waged an extensive and "secret" anti-Republican shipping campaign. The Italians did not modify their operations until their submarines fired clearly identifiable Italian torpedoes up on the beaches at Barcelona and Tarragona and a combined French and British naval force threatened to sink these "unknown" submarines as part of the Nyon Agreement.[41] (See separate entry on the Nyon Agreement on page 21.)

The Soviet Union also wanted to get a foothold in Spain. The Spanish Communist Party was very well organized and led. It had more than 250,000 members at the outbreak of the war and dominated all of the other political parties in the Republican government. The Spanish Communist Party saw the Nationalists as a reactionary threat to democracy and sided with the Republican government. The Soviet government initially did not get materially involved in the war, but became frustrated with the significant "disguised" "non-interventionist" involvement of Germany and Italy. The Soviets hoped that the French would aid the Republic more than they did but as Admiral Kuznetsov stated, "The Soviet Union alone displayed warm sympathy from the start."[42] In the fall of 1936 the Soviet Union started supplying the Republic with a significant amount of material (sent via ship) and eventually more than 2000 "volunteers."[43]

America, like Great Britain and France, remained officially neutral during the Spanish Civil War. The US government, by remaining neutral denied vital war materials to the legitimate Republican government. The Republican government attempted to obtain war materials from the US, but the Neutrality Act was updated by Congress to preclude the shipment of war materials to Spain. America remained neutral during the war at the urging of the Secretary of State, Cordell Hull. America's neutrality was driven by a desire to remain outside of European politics so as to avoid entanglement in what could become a general European war and a strong desire to maintain close relations with Great Britain and France to preserve associated collective security arrangements. As Guttman persuasively argues, though, for a subset of society there was a level of sympathy for Franco (including many American Catholics). There was also a concern that a left-of-center government in Spain could be a threat to significant American business interests in Latin America (some $3 billion in investments in 1936). Once America embarked on a policy of neutrality during the war, it never varied from it. At the conclusion of the war some American leaders that had been for neutrality realized that they might have condemned a legitimate elected government to being overthrown. President

Roosevelt when talking with the US Ambassador to Spain in March 1939, Claude G. Bowers (Bowers was a strong advocate of intervention on behalf of the Republic), said with regard to neutrality, "We have made a mistake; you have been right all along."[44]

EARLY COOPERATION AMONG THE NAVAL POWERS IN THE SPANISH CIVIL WAR; THE EVACUATION OF THE NON-COMBATANTS

One of the most interesting stages of the Spanish Civil War was the evacuation of non-combatants by the navies of Great Britain, France, Germany, Italy and the United States. The navies cooperated well with each other to save as many of the refugees of the war as possible. The level of cooperation and professionalism was truly remarkable. It was hoped by the officers and crews of the ships involved at the time that all would continue to work together and remain neutral in the fullest sense. Unfortunately, the cooperative spirit and camaraderie that developed between the ships of the various navies involved did not outlast the short duration refugee crisis from July to November 1936.[45]

At the start of the war there were approximately 100,000 foreigners some 84,000 who resided in Spain plus a large number of tourists, all caught up in the whirlwind of the war. Foreigners who for whatever reason found themselves in the wrong zone, could be in great jeopardy. The 17,000 French citizens, a number of who were domestic servants, were particularly vulnerable if they were in a Republican controlled city. Foreign residents of Spain also included 15,000 Germans, 4000 Italians, 4000 Argentines, 8000 British, and 1500 American citizens. Approximately 22,000 of the foreigners lived in the vicinity of Barcelona and another 8000 in Madrid.[46]

The refugees that fled to the ports for evacuation had numerous horror stories about the rough treatment they and others had received from the Republicans. The sailors themselves could see the death and destruction that took place in the vicinity of the Republican ports. British Royal Navy sailors watched as Republican ships shelled Malaga. Others saw burnt out churches in the towns, barricades and met with the Republican officials who were unshaven and discourteous. They observed the prison ships in the Republican harbor of Barcelona and saw crowded cars driven up to the hill to the prison barracks in Barcelona and heard the shots fired after the "trial" of the victim. The Nationalists, too, were guilty of wanton death and destruction, but they waged their "war" further inland. Consequently, the foreign navies tended to favor the Nationalists over the Republicans.[47]

The British had the first ships on scene for evacuation. The ships were sent "for the protection of British residents and visitors" on 20 July.[48] During the first three months of the evacuation, thirty-one ships were involved. The ships steamed a total of 97,000 miles in three months and carried more than six thousand refugees to safety. Of the six thousand, only two thousand were British citizens.[49] Other navies became rapidly involved with ships "pier side" including the Italians on 20 July, the French on 21 July, followed by the Germans and the Americans. The number of German and Italian ships involved in evacuating refugees was significant. The Germans deployed a large portion of their Navy, including the "pocket battleships" *Deutschland* and *Admiral Scheer*, the cruiser *Koln*, plus six torpedo boats. The Germans and Italians maintained a significant naval presence in Spanish waters for the remainder of the war and would periodically rotate their ships through for training.[50]

There was unhesitating cooperation among the foreign warships during the refugee crisis, as they evacuated refugees regardless of nationality who could somehow make it "pier side." The warships cooperated so well together for a number of reasons including: the sense of urgency and shared danger, the common purpose, and similar assessment of the Spanish political situation. During the course of the war there was the ever-present threat of mines and of being mistakenly attacked. On 5 August 1936, in Algerciras Bay the British destroyer *Basilisk* came under attack by the Nationalist gunboat *Dato*, who mistook her for the Republican destroyer *Alcala Galliano* with whom she had recently engaged. The British ship hoisted a large ensign but was bracketed by gunfire before the mistake was realized. The Nationalists apologized profusely.[51]

The officers of all ships definitely shared an aversion to the Republican officers. The elimination of the officer corps in the Republican Navy was well known among the foreign officers who preferred to deal with their aristocratic counterparts in the Nationalist Navy. The disparate navies quickly resolved communication difficulties. France made her harbors available to the foreign warships and even made her naval bases available for emergency repairs. The Germans and Italians were able to take advantage of the British naval base at Gibraltar. On 19 August 1936 British, German, and Italian warships sortied from Palma de Mallorca when the Republicans threatened to commence a naval bombardment of the port while a German merchant ship, *Hero*, continued to evacuate refugees. In the face of the multi-national sortie, the Republicans backed down. This cooperation among the foreign navies was not to last. Balance of power political considerations soon intruded. [52]

The foreign navies ended up evacuating between eighty and ninety percent of the refugees. The navies that participated in the refugee crisis benefited in many ways. The refugees showed much gratitude towards their rescuers. One lady was heard to remark when disembarking in Marseilles, "These men are not sailors; they are angels."[53] Another story concerned one of the officers on a destroyer who volunteered to get an infant down a steep ladder while the parents, who knew no English stood by. As the officer began to descend the ladder the baby began to scream. The officer remarked, "If you don't stop that XXX noise I'll wring your XXX neck!" The child froze in silence and the parents remarked what wonderful parenting skills the officer had![54]

The Italian and German officers were comparatively "new on the block" compared to the officers of the French, British and American navies. They most strongly desired to be treated and respected as equals which they were during the refugee crisis. Friendships were formed by the officers from different navies while the crews of the navies got to know each other very well during the crisis. A level of trust was built up between them. The Germans and Italians appear to have been well intentioned during the crisis. As Frank so well notes though, the refugee crisis acted as a false front while the German and Italian Navies protected their merchant shipping. The merchant ships that were protected delivered critical war material to the Nationalists that eventually allowed them to win. The Italians were even able to secure a base in Palma de Mallorca in the midst of the refugee crisis.[55]

Had the Germans and Italians not had the refugee evacuation to serve as the proverbial "camels nose in the tent," their direct intervention in the war would have been much more difficult to hide and the political stakes would have been higher. The refugee crisis allowed the Germans and Italians to gradually build up forces and become more heavily involved without unduly alarming the British and French. It can also be shown that a number of senior officers maintained friendships and an aversion to the Republicans despite their governments declared neutrality even after it became obvious that the Germans and Italians were not neutral. Once the Italian and German ships were in Spanish waters for humanitarian needs it was more difficult to declare them as not being neutral and eject them from Spanish waters. As long as German and Italian participation on the Nationalist side was not precipitously overt, the war would percolate well along before the French, British, and Americans became concerned enough to revisit their declared stance of neutrality in the war.[56]

GERMANY AND THE NATIONALIST NAVY

One of the most important factors in the Nationalists' eventual victory in the Spanish Civil War was the direct and decisive involvement of the German Navy. Prior to the coup being initiated, it was anticipated that the Nationalists would be able to move out quickly and that within a few short days Spain would be theirs. Much of Spain, including cities such as Madrid and Barcelona, remained in the Republicans hands and the coup degenerated into a war of attrition. The Nationalists quickly used up their own resources and had to rely on external powers to supply them. Hitler did not want the Nationalists to lose, but he also did not want them to win too quickly. It was important to him that the France and Great Britain remain preoccupied with the Civil War while he solidified his gains in the East, i.e., the Austrian Anschluss. The more turmoil that was created, the greater Hitler's geopolitical freedom and it gave him time to rebuild the military. Germany would keep Spain at the boiling point and provide enough material to eventually allow the Nationalists to win. The German Supreme Naval Command, Oberkommando der Marine (OKM), did not understand Hitler's logic and the far-reaching strategic goals that he had in mind. They thought he made a purely emotional decision to support Franco (after attending an opera by Wagner or something like that.). Despite the OKM's and other's misgivings, Germany moved out quickly to support Franco.[57]

In one of Germany's first overt acts of support for the Nationalists, on 24 July 1936, a German squadron commanded by Rear Admiral Carls that included *Deutschland* and *Admiral Scheer* departed Wilhelmshaven and arrived in Ceuta, Spanish Morocco on 3 August. Carls inspected the Spanish Legionnaires and Moors that were assembled in his honor and met with Franco and a number of other leaders of the Nationalists. The visit of the ships received wide publicity. To further solidify the relationship, when *Deutschland* departed Ceuta, *Deutschland* screened Ceuta from the Republican battleship *Jaime I* that had come to shell the city. *Jamie I* departed without firing a shot.[58]

Germany never had less than 50 percent of her Navy in Spanish waters supporting Franco. Germany had typically two of her three "pocket battleships," four of six cruisers, one torpedo boat flotilla and as many as four submarines (The subs operated west of Gibraltar) deployed to support the war. It was a considerable burden for the "new" German Navy to bear, but they were very innovative in keeping the navy at sea. The first phase of German operations had two goals, to protect German merchant shipping and to evacuate German nationals wherever threatened. The previous chapter discussed the evacuation of foreign nationals; the protection of merchant shipping is worth looking at more closely.[59]

The Republic declared all ports controlled by the Nationalists a war zone. By declaring a war zone, the Republic disclaimed all responsibility for loss or damage to warships or merchants that entered these ports. The Republic hoped that by declaring ports a war zone, that they could strangle the Nationalists. From an international law perspective, for the war zone/blockade to be effective, the Republican Navy would have to be able to enforce it. The British and Americans said that the Republican Navy was not capable of enforcing the blockade; therefore they would not recognize it. They did not want to recognize the blockade because it would grant belligerent rights to the Republic. If the Spanish Republic were to be granted belligerent rights, the Nationalists would be able to say that they too could establish a blockade of the ports they controlled and should also be accorded belligerent rights. It may have been coincidental that the Spanish Republican government would first try to enforce a blockade in a series of incidents with German merchant shipping. The incidents included Republican ships firing at and seizing German merchant ships. The Germans at first responded tepidly, but after the first few incidents they dispatched warships to protect their ships. They also ensured that their merchant shipping, especially those that were carrying "special" cargos (contraband) had explicit instructions on when and how to enter port and means to communicate with German warships.[60]

The Germans were particularly sensitive about the potential intercept of "special steamers" that they used to transport contraband. They desired to minimize the visibility of what they were doing to aid Franco so as to not unduly agitate the British and French. By all of the international non-intervention conventions, these "special steamers" were very much carrying contraband and could be seized. Per OKM's recommendation once the ships were in the vicinity of the Nationalist ports force protection for them would be the responsibility of the Nationalist Navy. For OKM's recommendation to be effective, a good deal of coordination would have to take place between the Nationalists and the Germans. Essentially, a combined naval staff would have to be formed. The Nationalists, though, did not take kindly to orders from the Germans and at first the Germans and Nationalists were unable to overcome their cross-cultural differences.[61]

The arrangement was tested when in December of 1936, the German "special steamer" *Procida* was to enter the Nationalist controlled port of El Ferrol. The ships entered port without incident, but when she made her official report to OKM she noted, "*Procida* entered the Spanish north coast without escort and left the Spanish north coast without having seen one Spanish warship." The Nationalist Navy was overextended attempting to blockade Republican ports and since El Ferrol was the safest port for German shipping, they saw no need to provide an escort. From there after, the Germans would escort their own "special steamers."[62]

The Republicans seized a non-contraband "conventional" merchant, *Palos*, on 27 December 1936 in the vicinity of Bilbao. The Kriegsmarine considered the seizure of *Palos* to be illegal and reacted angrily. On 28 December 1936 the OKM authorized Rear Admiral Carls to seize Republican merchants as faustpfandnahme (pawns) to secure the release of *Palos*. The Republicans released the ship, but not the cargo and one Spanish crewmember. Eventually, the cargo and Spanish crewmember were released but not before the crisis escalated considerably. The Germans seized three merchant ships and made preparations to attack "red" merchant and naval vessels and shell "red" ports. Germany had moved in the span of four months from tepid/neutral involvement to nearly conducting a naval war against Republican interests. Had Germany attacked "red" shipping, the war may have very well expanded into the much-feared general European war.[63]

The German protection of their merchant shipping was very effective. In the next two years more than sixty merchant vessels were interfered with by surface vessels but none were German. The Germans firm resolve to let no one interfere with their shipping and to take dramatic measures to defend their shipping gave them de facto right to trade freely with the Nationalists. The German Navy next turned their sights on interfering with Republican merchants and naval vessels to help win the land battle.[64]

In October 1936, Rear Admiral Carls expanded and further delineated the missions of the German Navy in Spain in relative priority:

1. Protection and escort of "Sonderdampfer," special steamers, engaged in covert, priority trade with Insurgent ports.

2. Protection of German interests and German citizens.

3. Reconnaissance on behalf of the Insurgents and transmittal of intelligence thus developed to "Guido,'" the German staff at Franco's headquarters in Salamanca, later Burgos.

4. Reconnaissance for the purpose of gathering evidence about Russian shipments of war material to the Republic, for submission by German Foreign Office to the Nonintervention Committee in London.[65]

Germany had too many missions and too few warships. They needed to get the Nationalists more involved in the war to the extent could lessen the burden on the overextended German Navy. The solution was to strengthen and train the Nationalist Navy. The Germans had few ships themselves but they did provide training to the Nationalists. The Germans conducted extensive reconnaissance of Republican targets, but could not order/direct the Nationalists as to how to employ their forces. The Nationalists were not always receptive. The Germans were particularly frustrated with their erstwhile clients in the first year of the war. They had excellent intelligence, but the Nationalists repeatedly failed to act on their advice. Franco's counter-advice was the German Navy to, "torpedo every blacked-out ship north of Majorca." The Nationalists wanted the Germans to sink all neutral shipping bound for Barcelona. This was more involvement than the Germans wanted! The Germans could build up an extensive intelligence base and routinely closed Republican warships with their warships, but they could not attack. The Nationalists were unwilling to risk their small fleet against the larger Republican one.[66]

In the winter of 1936-1937 the Germans and Nationalists conducted a mining campaign of the Republic's Mediterranean coast. The Nationalists also mined the Republican ports of Bilbao, Santander and Gijon and Nationalist warships patrolled outside the harbor. On land, the Nationalist Army drove through the Republican controlled Basque Provinces and Asturias to the sea while the mines and Nationalist warships enforced a blockade. For the first time in the war, from a German perspective, the Nationalists had acted aggressively. The blockade and land campaign were very effective. The Basque Provinces and the Asturias fell to the Nationalists in June 1937. Unfortunately, for the Nationalists, the Nationalist battleship *Espana* wandered into one of the minefields and sank. The successes in the region allowed the Nationalists to shift ships to the western Mediterranean while continuing their mine campaign along the Republican coast.[67]

The mine campaign seemed like a good idea. The mines were more easily employed than submarines and dramatically limited shipping into ports. Unfortunately, the mines were also indiscriminant. The mines were "more than happy" to sink Italian, British, and French ships. Matters were further complicated in that the mines were casually laid and a number of them drifted. The Nationalists insisted upon using the mines. The Germans still endorsed mine warfare, but offered some recommendations for their employment. They even sent their mine supply ship home to encourage Franco to stop the mine campaign. Eventually, the political costs to Franco became too high in the conduct of the sea mine campaign. Franco was attempting to further legitimize his regime abroad, but his task was made much more difficult by the mines. The mine campaign was stopped, but not before a British merchant and destroyer were sunk, resulting in a diplomatic protest. Interestingly, at a meeting, Admiral Evans, the Commandant of Gibraltar, advised his German counterpart, Admiral von Fischel, that if the Nationalists really wanted to influence the course of the war that they should regularly bombard every Republican supply port. This would allow the supplies to the "reds" to be halted.[68]

After the mine campaign, the Nationalists moved into their next stage of the naval campaign, the Kreuzerkrieg, (cruiser war). The Nationalist warships would attack unarmed merchantmen and either bring them into port or sink them. The Nationalists did not start their campaign until December 1937. The Germans wanted them to start earlier, but the Italians were ably sinking numerous merchants with no risk to Nationalist warships. Also, the Nyon agreement had complicated matters and the Nationalists did not wish to risk a confrontation with the British or French until their interest in enforcing the agreement waned. The Nationalists sank and seized numerous ships, but the Germans knew that the Republicans were still being well supplied from the sea. The Nationalists avoided attacking British and French flagged ships, which the Republicans were using. Chief of the Nationalist blockade, Admiral Moreno, wanted to do more, but Franco explicitly ordered him not to take any further action against British and French ships. It was 1938 and the war was winding down. Franco was trying not to exacerbate his post-war relationships with the British and French any further.[69]

Tanner notes that the Germans thought that the Nationalists never employed their Navy as effectively as possible. Large numbers of merchants were sunk and seized, but the British and French continued to get supplies to the Republicans. That is true, but the post-war strategic construct that Franco was attempting to shape did not allow him to do more. Franco was trying to leave some links to the British and French in the post-hostilities phase of the conflict. The British and the French had preponderant naval forces in the Mediterranean. Should Franco become too bold for the sake of stopping some supplies, the British and French could move away from their official stance of "neutrality" and Franco's Navy would not stand a chance. More importantly, the Republicans would be even better supplied (Soviet and other merchants would be able to get through to the Republican ports once the Nationalist Navy was out of the picture) and the tide of the battle would shift on land. The Germans had already indicated that they were not willing to do more, like sink blacked out merchants and potentially expand the war. Franco would be on his own. He wisely chose the more reasonable course than his German friends advocated.

THE NYON AGREEMENT

The Republicans had been receiving significant material aid from the Soviet Union since November of 1936. During the first year of the war, the Soviets used the Republican controlled ports of Bilbao and Santander in the North of Spain, along the Bay of Biscay adjacent to the French border, to supply the Republicans. With the fall of Bilbao and Santander in the summer of 1937, the Soviets were forced to use ports in the Mediterranean to supply the Republicans.[70] The Soviets mainly used Republican vessels to ship arms to Spain and used British flagged ships for legitimate cargo that included oil, coal, food, and other supplies. On August 3, 1937 Franco made an urgent request to Mussolini to use the Italian fleet to prevent the passage of Soviet transports between Sicily and the North African coast. Franco went so far as to send his brother, Nicolas Franco, to ask Mussolini to do everything possible to stop Soviet shipping. According to Italian Foreign Minister Ciano, "the Duce was in principle still inclined to do everything he could to put a stop to them (the Soviet transports)- not with surface vessels to be sure, but only with submarines, in Sicilian waters: In case Italian submarines had to surface, they would display the Spanish flag." Franco's brother implored Mussolini to do even more than just use submarines to stop merchant ships carrying Soviet material and Mussolini agreed to use Italian surface ships too in the maritime campaign against the Soviets.[71]

The Italian Navy acted quickly on Mussolini's agreement with Franco to stop merchant vessels carrying Soviet war material. On the same day the agreement was made, 11 August 1937, the Spanish tanker *Campeador*, which had been followed during the day by two Italian destroyers was attacked and sunk at dusk. The ship was torpedoed with several men being lost. The Italians did not bother to pick up survivors; British merchantmen in the vicinity rescued them later. The Italians followed up by sinking a Spanish ship on 13 August and shelling a Panamanian ship off Tunis. Italy's unrestricted submarine campaign commenced on 12 August. The Italians attacked French, and Spanish ships and then sank three Soviet ships between 31 August and 2 September. The Italians torpedoed the British merchant *Woodford* on 2 September. The Italians also attacked merchant shipping from Majorca based aircraft. The Italians pressed their luck when the submarine *Iride* narrowly missed torpedoing the British destroyer *Havock* on 1 September.[72]

The British contemplated a range of options in reprisal for the Italian attack on the *Havock* (and the British did know it was an Italian attack for they had broken their code). Foreign Secretary Eden wanted to attack the Nationalist Navy. He advocated that the Royal Navy hunt and sink the Nationalist's largest warship, the cruiser *Canarias*. The Admiralty was appalled. The Admiralty did not want to do anything to worsen the relations with the Italians nor did they want to concentrate the fleet anymore than it was in the Western Mediterranean. The Royal Navy was over extended with Mediterranean commitments that included having ships in the Eastern Mediterranean on patrol should the Italians do anything precipitous in Libya that would threaten Egypt. In the end, Eden was able to convince British Prime Minister Chamberlain to have a conference on Mediterranean "piracy" and the British fleet was reinforced in the Western Mediterranean.[73]

An international naval conference was convened in Nyon, Switzerland on 10 September. France, Great Britain, Germany, Italy Yugoslavia, Albania, Greece, Turkey, Egypt, Russia, Romania, and Bulgaria were invited. It is important to note that at this stage the British and French did not officially know who was conducting the anti-shipping campaign. Italy and Germany were also invited to attend, but they promptly declined. The French and British naval staffs worked together to come up with an agreed upon policy prior to the conference. The French did not want their ships under the control of the British and the neither wanted the convoy system to be used. A fixed route system was developed for merchant ships to use that would be patrolled by destroyers and aircraft. The British wanted to act first against the submarine threat but the French wanted to attack both suspect surface ships and submarines. The British did not want to attack the surface ships because they did not want to worsen their relations with the Italians. Since the submarines were not known to be Italian, they could be attacked reasoned the British without directly confronting Italy. The British were very concerned about the Italians increasing political entanglement with the Germans. The British did what they could to keep the Italians and Germans separated.[74]

By the time the conference met on 10 September, British code breaking had revealed that the Nyon conference had already been successful; the Italians had broken off all offensive actions on 4 September. The Italians had stopped the campaign because of British and French protests and their determination to hold the conference. The British did not let anyone know including the French, that they were breaking the Italian codes. The Russians attended the conference and very much wanted to participate in the naval patrols. The British had only allowed the Russians to be invited at the insistence of the French. The French were afraid that if the Russians were not invited they would lose the support of the socialists and the French government would fall. The British had traditionally opposed any Russian naval expansion into the Mediterranean. The Russians wanted to help the Turks, Greeks, and Yugoslavs to patrol the Aegean Sea. Fortunately, the Turks, Greeks, and Yugoslavians could not agree to work with the Russians (to a certain extent they were aligned with Germany) and the Russians agreed to French and British patrols only in the Mediterranean.[75]

As a result of the conference, French and British cooperation increased significantly. The French allowed the British to operate within their territorial waters and for British ships and flying boats to be stationed in French harbors. After much discussion it was agreed that ships on patrol "were instructed to intervene to the limits of their power in the case in which a surface ship carried out an inhumane attack."[76] On 20 September the Nyon patrols started. The Nyon agreement saved the Republicans from disaster. The Nationalists were not happy. The Republicans could now be resupplied and the Nationalist submarines could not patrol outside of Spanish territorial waters for fear of being sunk by the destroyer patrols. The British and French pressed for Italian involvement in the patrols to keep the Italians from falling completely into the German sphere of influence. The Italians, who initially would not join the conference because the Russians were invited, now said they would not join the conference because the patrol zone that they were allocated was too small. The Nyon agreement was updated to include language to the effect that Italy was a great power and Italy then joined the parties in the Nyon agreement. It was a curious turn of events. The Italian representative to the conference, Ciano, noted, "From suspicious pirates to the policemen of the Mediterranean, and the Russians whose ships we were sinking excluded." On 10 November the Italians joined the patrols.[77]

The Nyon agreement is one of the few examples of successful multi-national cooperation in the Spanish Civil War. French and British cooperated as they rarely had in the past and important relationships were formed between the staffs that would well serve them in the build up to World War II. The Russians were able to resupply the Republicans and keep them from collapsing in 1937. The Italians were able to slow down the supplies the Russians were delivering to the Republic, sink a few vessels, and be declared a great power. Most importantly from a German perspective, the Italians were even now more firmly in the German sphere of influence. On the plus side for the British, they were able to take the measure of the Italian Navy during the war and found them to be wanting. The Italian Navy was relatively quickly eliminated as a threat to British interests at the start of World War II. Over time, Franco's Navy became more proficient and there was no need to rely on the Italians again to conduct unrestricted submarine warfare to slow down the Russian supplies. In conclusion, there is much that can be learned from the Nyon agreement, but tragically for the Republicans it only delayed their inevitable defeat. The Russians simply could not keep up with the supplies and personnel that the Italians and Germans provided to the Nationalists.

SOVIET UNION AND THE REPUBLICAN NAVY

The Soviets played a major role in the Spanish Civil War. They massively supplied the Republican government. Supplies included 806 combat aircraft, 362 tanks, 120 armored reconnaissance vehicles, 1555 artillery pieces, hundreds of thousands of small arms, torpedo boats, torpedoes and fuel. The supplies that the Soviets provided kept the Republicans in the war. The supplies were not given freely to the Republic, but came with "strings attached," 2000 Soviet advisers.[78]

The advisers played a key role in the war at times they assumed direct control over the employment of the military. In post-war analysis, the Soviets have been blamed in part for the downfall of the Republic. One Spanish Republican Army officer stated,

> I can affirm in all the operations in which I took part as an Army Commander, in order to find out anything about what aero planes and tanks were at my disposition, or how they could be tactically used, I always had to enter into direct relations with the "friendly advisers" and only sometimes with the Spanish Chiefs of Aviation and Tanks. Frequently during the carrying on of war operations, in order to have the support of aircraft, we had to change our timetable for one that they imposed, often with lamentable results.

This officer goes on to state that advisers stymied the development of a coherent campaign plan and the poor performance of the Communists and technicians was a major cause of the defeat of Republican forces.[79]

In fairness to the Soviets, the provision of supplies necessitated "strings." The material was power, both militarily and politically. The overall paucity of material and extended maritime supply line necessitated that the supplies be properly employed. Most importantly, for the land campaign the Soviet advisers played a crucial role and kept the Republicans from collapsing all together early on in the war. The Germans and Italian advisers were directly involved in helping Franco's Army, too, and prior to the Soviets' arrival they were winning on the ground. Furthermore, The Axis powers did not limit themselves to just providing advisers. Thousands of Italian soldiers fought on the side of Franco (greater than 50,000 has been estimated.) Within six months of the Soviet advisers arrival, a modern Italian Army was defeated at Guadalajara and Franco's advance was slowed down. The Soviets organized, trained and directed the effective employment of identical Republican forces that had been losing without supplying a Soviet Army to fight for the Republic. The Soviet advisers direct involvement in the land campaign led to a truly remarkable turnaround for the Republic.[80]

The Soviets advisers' success on land was not duplicated at sea. If anything, the poor advice that the Soviets contributed significantly to the relative irrelevancy of the Republican navy to the course of the war. The war was first and foremost a war of logistics and associated lines of communication. The Nationalists had comparatively short-lines of communication (from Italy and Germany), whereas the Republic relied extensively on material provided from the Soviet Union. The material from the Soviet Union had to transit the Black Sea and the entire Mediterranean or be transported to France and cross the Pyrenees. Given that eighty to ninety percent of all supplies to participants in the war went by sea, anything that could be done to interdict the supply lines would have a significant impact on the war. The Soviet Union was first and foremost a land power. It will be shown that their unfamiliarity with what it takes to conduct an effective maritime campaign coupled with rigid doctrine resulted in poor advice to the Republican Navy and the eventual defeat of Republican forces on the ground.

Soviet naval theory before the Spanish Civil War was divided into two schools, the old school and the new school. Old school theorists took a Mahanian view of naval power, that battleships and cruisers were essential to maritime control of the high seas and the approaches to Soviet waters. Submarines were viewed as a threat to sea lines of communication but submarines in and of themselves were not enough to protect your own lines of communication. The Soviet Union did not have the resources to build the high-seas fleet that the old school required in the 1920's and many of the old school theorists were also purged. In 1923, Professor M. Petrov postulated a new school of naval theory. He theorized in this new school that an "active" (offensive) defense by small naval forces was required to control the coastal approaches to the Soviet Union. These small naval forces (submarines, patrol boats, etc.) would be supported by land-based aircraft. By 1925 this new school "active" defense was the accepted naval strategy in the Soviet Union. The Soviet Union concentrated on the build-up of a Navy that consisted of submarines, PT boats, high-speed destroyers, and naval aircraft but no battleships, aircraft carriers or cruisers. In the new school, the submarine was the capital ship and the striking arm of the fleet. This naval theory may have been suitable for a land power such as the Soviet Union, but for a nation that traditionally relied on the sea such as Spain it would prove to be a disastrous.[81]

From October 1936 to November 1938 the Soviet advisers essentially controlled the Republican Navy. Whatever "advice" they gave was actually an order to the Republican Navy. The Soviets had the Republicans utilize their "active" defense doctrine for the employment of the Republican fleet. The doctrine should not have been used for the Republican Navy could have been used to decisively influence events at sea. The Republican fleet was twice as large as the Nationalist fleet but it was only used in the vicinity of Republican ports and to escort ships. Soviet merchants and other supply vessels were only escorted when they were typically less than 150 miles from Spain. While the vessels were en route to Spain they were subjected to submarine "piracy," effective air attack by the Italians, Germans and Nationalists in addition to being intercepted by surface ships. In stark contrast, the Nationalists aggressively employed their naval forces to control the seas. The Nationalists ensured their own supply lines were safe and subjected Republican ports and shipping to periodic attack.[82]

Specific examples of poor Soviet naval advice to the Republicans are numerous. The examples range from individual attacks on ships of the Republican Navy to allowing the Italians and Nationalists to gain and keep control of Majorca. Indalecio Prieto, Minister of the Republican Navy, stated that he ordered the movement of the destroyer *Ciscar* across the Strait of Gibraltar from its anchorage at Gijon. The chief of the Soviet advisers asked Prieto to revoke his order. Prieto refused, but a local Communist agent on scene kept the ship from sailing and it was sunk. When the Soviets could have stepped in and prevented the Republicans from making poor decisions they did not. Prieto, no naval strategist, was allowed to order the evacuation of Republican militiamen from Catalonia who had established a beachhead in Majorca in September 1936. The militiamen were on the verge of victory when they were withdrawn in the face of weak Nationalist and Italian opposition. The Italians quickly built up forces on Majorca and dominated the western Mediterranean from then on.[83]

The nadir for Soviet advice was when they did not intervene to keep the Republican fleet from redeploying from the Mediterranean to the Bay of Biscay to support Republican land forces. The Nationalists only had one cruiser, the *Almirante Cevera* that was harassing shipping in the vicinity of the Bay of Biscay and Bilbao. The Republicans only left a few destroyers to control the Strait of Gibraltar. Prior to redeploying the ships on 3 September 1936, Prieto consulted with his Soviet naval adviser, Captain N.G. Kuznetsov, who raised no objections. Kuznetsov only later realized the significant blunder he had made. Kuznetsov stated in his autobiography,

> During the first few months after the revolt Franco's ships would not venture out to sea. It was only the Italian airlift that helped the insurgents bring troops from Africa. Perhaps joining hands with the land forces the Republican fleet could attempt to seize the ports of Gibraltar. This would have affected the entire course of the war. But, alas ... the fleet sailed to the north."[84]

The Nationalist fleet quickly redeployed to dominate the Strait of Gibraltar. On 29 September, Captain Francisco Moreno arrived in the Strait with the Nationalist cruisers *Almirante Cevera* and *Canarias* surprising and easily defeating the remaining Republican defenders. The Battle of Cape Spartel was the culminating point in the naval war. The Republican Navy would from then on be a "fleet in being" that would never again seriously challenge Nationalist control of the seas.[85]

Given control of the seas, the Nationalists quickly moved additional men and material from Spanish Morocco to Spain. Eight thousand soldiers of the Army of Africa were shuttled via ship to Spain in a few days and eventually as many as 50,000 men would arrive in Spain from Spanish Morocco via ship. Nine out of every ten soldiers that fought in the battle for Madrid for Franco came from Spanish Morocco. Vital American oil that was being shipped to the Canary Islands for Franco could now be sent to rebel controlled ports in Spain. The Nationalists were able to secure their hold on Majorca, never to lose the island for the remainder of the war. The Republican fleet straggled back into Cartagena and remained there. The Republicans formulated a plan to regain control of the Strait of Gibraltar and to seize Majorca, but it was rejected by the Soviets.[86]

The Nationalists and their Fascist allies mounted an increasingly aggressive campaign as the war progressed against Soviet supplied material. Initially, the officers of the Nationalist Navy were not certain they could rely on their crews and the Republican Navy was too strong in the vicinity of Spain for the Nationalists to wage an effective guerre de course campaign without unduly risking their smaller Navy.[87] Accordingly, they relied upon the Italians and Germans to interdict as much shipping as possible before it reached Spain. A combination of submarines, surface ships and aircraft were used to interdict shipping with increasing success. Italian and German aircraft were particularly proficient. From the end of the Italian submarine campaign with the Nyon agreement in September 1937 to the end of the war Italian and German aircraft sank 115 and 51 foreign merchant ships respectively. These ships represented about three-fourths of all the shipping the Italians and Germans were able to sink during the war.[88]

Kuznetsov and his 76 fellow naval advisers simply could not come up with an effective strategy to counter that of the Nationalists and their Axis allies. The Republicans had a more powerful fleet than the Nationalists, but it was not used except for convoy escort. The Republican battleship *Jamie I* was allowed to be a useless floating battery off Almeria. Kuznetsov even advised that the cruiser *Miguel de Cervantes* and battleship *Jamie I* should be shifted from being pier-side in Cartagena to an exposed anchorage off Cartagena. They were then subjected to Nationalist submarine attack with the *Miguel de Cervantes* being damaged badly enough to be out of action for most of the war.[89]

The Soviet attempts to develop an effective naval air interdiction campaign were equally disastrous. Kuznetsov and Prieto wanted Soviet SB-2 medium bombers to help interdict shipping. When he finally did get the planes they had a very difficult time identifying targets, particularly the nationality of the shipping. In May 1937 untrained Soviet pilots mistakenly attacked an Italian auxiliary and the German "pocket battleship" *Deutschland*. This attack was a major international incident and the Germans shelled Almeria in reprisal.[90] In a meeting of the Republican Cabinet, Prieto sought to enlarge the war to a full European conflict. Prieto proposed that the Republican Navy seek out the German squadron for combat. Fortunately, cooler heads prevailed in the Spanish Cabinet and they appealed to world opinion about the heinous attack by the Germans on the "open city" of Almeria. Significantly, the Republican Navy would now act with much greater restraint in the vicinity of German ships. The Germans now had new rules of engagement that allowed them to attack any Republican ship, submarine or aircraft that approached a German ship.[91]

The inability of the Soviets to properly employ the Republican fleet was further exacerbated by the poor state of their own Navy. The Soviet government attempted to ready a naval force to defend their own supply ships. The force was to include the Soviet cruiser *Krasnyi Kavkaz* (a ship that Kuznetsov had previously been executive officer of in 1933[92]) and several destroyers and deploy to the Western Mediterranean to protect the ships. The warships were in such a sorry material condition and in a poor state of training that the project was quickly cancelled. The doctrine of "active" defense and financial constraints had kept the Soviets from building a Navy that could conduct anything but coastal defense prior to the Spanish Civil War. During that war the Soviets had to rely on others to protect their shipping. Stalin recognized the need for an open ocean Mahanian-style navy, but there was no time to build the fleet prior to World War II. During World War II The Soviets would again have to rely on others to protect their supply lines.[93]

Kuznetsov himself readily acknowledged that the Soviets failed from a naval perspective during the war:

> Throughout the events in Spain... we were unable to play a proper role in the naval control, conducted pursuant to a decision of the "Committee of Non-Intervention," because we lacked the necessary warships and logistics support ships. At the time it became particularly apparent how important the sea is for us and how we need a strong Navy. [94]

More important than the lack of ships though was the unsound "active" defense strategy. The Republican Navy was large enough to become a factor. All it needed was an effective doctrine and some training. The Soviets, if they had the right doctrine could have fought the Spanish war effectively by proxy (with the Republican Navy) without necessarily needing a fleet of their own. Kuznetsov thought that the main job of the Republican Navy was escort duty, not meeting the Nationalist fleet on the high seas and defeating it. Failure to confront the Nationalists on the high seas or in the air meant that the Nationalists could pick and chose when and where to concentrate forces to defeat the Republicans.[95]

The best condemnation of the active "defense" strategy comes from the Soviets themselves. Admiral Gorshkov, former Commander in Chief of the Soviet Navy stated:

> At the end of the 1930's the Soviet state set out on the course of creating a high seas fleet capable of resolving tasks at a significant distance from their bases. Powerful capital ships were laid down; the fleets received new cruisers, destroyers, long-range submarines, and other ships. But the lag of our military-theoretical thinking behind the steady increase of the strength of the Navy, the adherence to the previous (young school) views of its (the Navy's) use near the coasts which had been worked out in the period of the Navy's rehabilitation continued to constitute a hindrance which retarded the growth of our military strength.

Admiral Gorshkov goes on to say that the Soviets failed to learn the lesson about the importance of naval aviation (and build aircraft carriers) and that even though the Soviets did build a fleet, they could do nothing with it because they could not protect it from the air except when it operated close to base.[96]

28

If the Soviets had an effective naval doctrine, the Spanish Civil War may have turned out differently or, as Frank noted, at least last six months longer and merge with World War II. If the war had merged with World War II, Franco would have been another Fascist enemy who could have been confronted and defeated in kind. For example, if the Soviets had a Navy that could operate on the high seas, or if it had been able to direct the employment of the Republican Navy effectively, the Soviets could have kept the supply line though the Bay of Biscay open to the forces of the Republic. When the Northern Front collapsed under the combined onslaught of the Nationalist and Axis forces on land as they pushed to sea through the Asturias and Basque Provinces and the Nationalist Navy operated off the coast with impunity, it was the beginning of the end for the Republic. All the Soviets could do was appeal to the French and British Navies to protect their shipping which the British and French refused to do. Consequently, the Soviets watched while their merchant ships were either seized or sunk.[97]

In the last year of the war, the supply lines through the Mediterranean were so untenable that the Soviets ceased shipping supplies through the Mediterranean altogether. The Soviets used French ports and the French rail system, but the cargo could only cross the French-Spanish frontier with the permission of the French Cabinet. As a result, the border to Spain was not always open. During the final battle for Catalonia (December 1938-February 1939), large stockpiles of aircraft, tanks, torpedo boats and artillery pieces were held up on the French-Spanish border because the French Cabinet would not agree to open the border. If the Republican forces had access to these supplies, the war could have been prolonged. [98]

ENDURING LESSONS FROM THE SPANISH CIVIL WAR

The Victors Learn Few Lessons

In general, the Italian Navy performed poorly during the war. Their submarine campaign resulted in very few successful attacks on merchant shipping. The Italian Navy was primarily employed for convoy escort. The successes that the Italians had at sea (in the face of no overt threat) led them to believe that their material, doctrine, and training were sound. Unfortunately for the Italians, the British were able to take their measure with devastating results for the Italians at the start of World War II: decimating their submarines from June to July 1940 followed by their surface navy suffering defeats at Punta Stilo, Cape Spada, Taranto, and Cape Matapan.[99]

Unrestricted Submarine Warfare is Never Covert

The Italians conducted "covert" submarine warfare that was quickly discovered once ships began sinking. The submarine campaign was fraught with consequences. Had the British been willing to show greater resolve (for the French were certainly willing to help the Republic of Spain in a more open manner) the Italians, French and British may have found themselves involved in a naval war.

Need for Anti-Air Defenses and Air Supremacy

One of the real doctrinal winners in the Spanish Civil War was aviation in general and aviation in support of a war at sea in particular. The Germans and Italians waged a very successful anti-shipping campaign against merchant shipping using aircraft. There was never much of an anti-surface combatant campaign during the war using aircraft causing naval officers from all countries to assume that a surface combatant underway had little to fear from aviation. Consequently, shipboard anti-aircraft defense improvements were neglected prior to World War II.[100]

German and Italian aircraft sank ships that were unescorted and not in a convoy. The efficacy of the convoy system was demonstrated but the lesson did not take and the convoy system was not used initially during World War II resulting in critical losses. Kuznetsov understood the need for air supremacy, "Unless you have air supremacy, you can not gain supremacy on the sea."[101] But, the Soviet Navy was not able to make the changes in force structure and training prior to the start of World War II to employ the Soviet fleet effectively. The Americans were the only ones to conduct a fleet battle problem that utilized a similar scenario to that of the Spanish Civil War with aircraft and aircraft carriers at sea in support of a war in the littoral.[102]

Law of Unintended Consequences is Still in Effect

The *Deutschland* incident (when Soviet SB-2's mistakenly bombed the German warship) very nearly turned the Spanish Civil War into a European-wide conflict. The Soviets were merely looking for a diversion when the air attack was conducted. The Soviets hoped that by attacking Fascist cruisers (that were believed to be part of the Nationalist Navy) in the vicinity of Mallorca that the Republican Navy would be able to escort merchant vessels carrying Soviet supplies into port without interference. The supplies did get into port, but the Germans later ended up shelled Almeria in reprisal.[103]

Early Cooperation on Humanitarian Issues Can Mask War-Like Acts

The Germans and Italians used the refugee evacuation as a subterfuge to flow forces into theater and establish cordial working relationships with France, Great Britain, and America. Once the forces were in theater and in Spanish territorial waters, it was very difficult to eject them. The naval assets were then gradually able to more actively support the Nationalists without unduly alarming the British or French. Interests included protection of "special" merchant ships containing contraband and maintenance of a naval intelligence network that apprised Franco of the location of high interest shipping.[104]

Military Success is not the Same as Political Success

Militarily, the Italian submarine campaign was not particularly effective because a few ships were sunk. Politically, the submarine campaign was very effective because the Soviets stopped using the Mediterranean to ship supplies to the Republic. The Germans wanted the Nationalists to wage a much more aggressive anti-merchant ship campaign to choke off supplies to the Republic. Many more supply ships could have been sunk, but these would have been French and British flagged merchants. Franco wisely concluded that he could not count on the more dominant British and French Navies to stand idly by while he sunk their merchants with impunity. British and French naval involvement in the war would have jeopardized Franco's sea lines of communication.

Everyone is Always Willing to Fight an Enemy with Your Military Despite the Political Consequences to You

Franco very much wanted the Germans to sink merchant ships of all countries to cut off supplies to the Republic. Had the Germans acted, as Franco desired, in all likelihood a general European war would have broken out. Contrarily, the Germans wanted Franco to sink all merchant ships that were supplying the Republic, which would have led to the French and British interdicting Nationalist maritime supply lines.

No Amount of Material Can Make Up for Poor Doctrine

The Soviet "active" defense naval employment doctrine was neither. The Nationalist Navy, with the help of the Germans and Italians, were able to pick and chose the "fights" they wanted while the Republican Navy remained in a near pure "reactive" mode. Mahanian doctrine was validated. The Nationalists were able to establish an effective blockade and defeat the Republicans on the high seas. The Republic's failure to confront the Nationalists on the high seas because of their reliance on the Soviets for advice was a major reason why the Republicans lost. The Republican Navy was two times larger than the Nationalist Navy, yet once the Soviets began advising the Republicans, in was never again used decisively at sea.[105]

There is a Necessity to Define Ends Clearly and Revisit Periodically

For the British and Americans, once the non-interventionist policy was set, it was never revisited. The German and Italian intentions were initially unclear but it rather quickly became obvious that they had intervened to support Franco. The British and French could have taken a variety of escalatory actions to rein in the Germans and Italians that would be short of fermenting a general European war. Great Britain, though, was attempting to appease the Germans and the French and Americans linked their policy to that of the British.

Don't Kill the People That Learned the Lessons from the War

The Soviets failed to learn from the Spanish Civil War. The Soviets sent their best and brightest as advisers to Spanish Republic including Ian Karlovich Berzin former head of the Intelligence Directorate of the Red Army who served as Chief Military Advisor. The head of the Red Army, Marshal M.N. Tukhachevsky, sponsor of Soviet Field Regulations, PU-1936, which articulated the concept of deep battle and deep operations, aggressively tried to learn from the Spanish Civil War and revise doctrine accordingly. Deep operations doctrine was revised to reflect the need for Red Army officers to lead partisan detachments to attack enemy supply lines in the rear of the attacking force. Unfortunately, a series of purges were conducted in the Soviet military from 1937-1938 and sponsors of new doctrine such as Tukhachevsky and distinguished veterans of the war such as Berzin were purged and their ideas discredited.[106]

One of the few people not purged from 1937-1938 was then Captain Kuznetsov. He eventually advanced to be CinC of the Soviet Navy. Given his emphasis on building ships and not revising doctrine, it can could be argued that Kuznetsov's failure to learn and apply lessons from the war doomed the Soviet Navy to irrelevancy for decades. Soviet doctrine never really moved far away from the concept of "active" defense. Stalin had fully intended to build a blue water Navy at the end of World War II as he had learned the necessity of a large blue water Navy from the Spanish Civil War, but he died and his ideas fell into disfavor until the ascendancy of Admiral Gorshkov.[107]

CONCLUSION

If a nation depends on the seas at all, its sea lines of communication must be secure. If an enemy controls the seas of a littoral nation, he can pick and chose when and where to interdict maritime supply lines. In the Spanish Civil War, the unreliability of the French border crossings made maintenance of sea lines of communications vital to the Republican cause. The failure of the Republicans to control the sea lines of communications doomed the Republican Army to defeat on the battlefield. The Germans and Italians enthusiastically backed the Nationalists, supplying material and interfering with Republican merchant shipping with great effectiveness. As in tennis, they were more than willing to "work the chalk lines" with respect to aiding and abetting the Nationalists while not triggering precipitous involvement of Britain, France or the United States.

The Republican's inability to operate their Navy effectively was further exacerbated by the poor state of training and doctrine. When the Republican sailors overthrew the right-of-center officer corps, centuries of knowledge and training on how a great power should employ a Navy were lost. Unlike the Republican Army, almost the entire officer corps was destroyed. Consequently, when the Soviets provided military advisers to the Republic in August 1936, there was a leadership vacuum and the sailors, when they did have some good ideas on how to employ the Navy, were at a significant relative rank disadvantage. A former cook now in command of a warship had a difficult time in a discussion on tactics with a Soviet captain. As has been shown, the Russians "active" defense doctrine was not suited to Spain and should not have been forced upon the Republican Navy. The sailors did not have the "rank" to stand up to the Soviet advisers.

Franco won the Spanish Civil War and under his leadership Spain managed to stay on the sidelines during World War II. Spain was aligned with the Axis during the war and was able to take advantage of its "neutrality," i.e., ore sales to Germany, but Germany was never given access to Gibraltar (that Hitler was so desirous of), which would been a decisive point, allowing the entrance to the Mediterranean to be controlled. Spain was the only Fascist state to survive World War II because with the onset of the "Cold War" the US and its allies very much wanted to keep Spain in the Western sphere of influence. Spain granted access to the US for bases and Spain was admitted to the UN in 1954. But, in many respects it would have been better for Spain if it had lost World War II. Spain was a "prize" that was never contested for by the Allies. Given Franco's abilities at triangulation, the only way to get Spain to lose during World War II would have been if the Spanish Civil War did not end prior to the start of World War II. The Republic's inability to control the seas limited the material that Republican Spain had to fight on land and correspondingly (at a minimum) prolong the war. Had a Nationalist leaning Spain still been contested for between the Allies and the Axis, the Nationalists no doubt would have lost World War II. Had Spain lost World War II, Spain would have most likely been included in the Marshall Plan. Spain's economy would have progressed smartly and Spain would have had a democratic government more than thirty years earlier.

Word count: 15,588

ENDNOTES

[1] Anthony Beevor, <u>The Spanish Civil War</u> (New York, NY: Peter Bedrick Books, 1983), 8-11.

[2] Ibid.,11.

[3] Allen Guttmann, <u>Problems in American Civilization</u> (Boston, MA: DC Heath and Company, 1963), 91.

[4] Beevor, 11.

[5] Ibid., 15.

[6] Ibid., 15-18

[7] Ibid., 19.

[8] Ibid., 20-21.

[9] Ibid., 25.

[10] Ibid., 27-30.

[11] Ivan Maisky, <u>Spanish Notebooks</u> (London, England: Hutchinson of London, 1966), 15.

[12] Beevor, 31-38.

[13] Ibid., 39-41.

[14] Ibid., 43.

[15] Ibid., 43-47.

[16] Ibid., 47.

[17] Ibid., 48.

[18] Hugh Thomas, <u>The Spanish Civil War</u> (New York, NY: Harper & Row, 1977), 140-144.

[19] Beevor, 51-53.

[20] Ibid., 62.

[21] Ibid., 62-63.

[22] Thomas, 243.

[23] Stephen W. Roskill, <u>Naval Policy Between the Wars: The Period of Reluctant Reamament, 1930-1939</u> (Annapolis, MD: Naval Institute Press, 1976), 370.

[24] Peter Eslob, <u>Condor Legion</u> (New York, NY: Ballantine Books, 1973), 52.

[25] Stephen William Tanner, <u>German Naval Intervention in the Spanish Civil War as Reflected by the German Records</u> (Washington, DC: The American University Library, 1976), 55.

[26] Kenneth Edwards, <u>The Grey Diplomastists</u> (London, England: Rich and Cowan, Ltd., 1938), 248.

[27] Tanner, 176.

[28] Roskill, 370.

[29] Robert H. Whealey, <u>Hitler and Spain: the Nazi Role in the Spanish Civil War, 1936-1939</u> (Lexington, KY: University Press of Kentucky, 1989), 3.

[30] Whealey, 13.

[31] Ibid., 13

[32] Lawrence W. Pratt, <u>East of Malta, West of Suez: Britain's Mediterranean Crisis, 1936-1939</u> (Cambridge, London: Cambridge University Press, 1975), 42.

[33] Dante A. Puzzo, <u>Spain and the Great Powers, 1936-1941</u> (New York, NY: Columbia University Press, 1962), 73.

[34] Pratt, 63-65.

[35] Robert J. Young, <u>In Command of France: French Foreign Policy and Military Planning, 1934-1940</u> (Cambridge, MA: Harvard University Press, 1978), 135-138.

[36] Whealey, 15.

[37] Puzzo, 63.

[38] Brian R. Sullivan, "Fascist Italy's Military Involvement in the Spanish Civil War," <u>Journal of Military History</u> 59 (October 1995): 702.

[39] John F. Coverdale, <u>Italian Intervention in the Spanish Civil War</u> (Princeton, NJ: Princeton University Press, 1975), 28-37.

[40] Willard C. Frank, "Politico-Military Deception at Sea in the Spanish Civil War, 1936-1939," <u>Intelligence and National Security</u> 5 (July 1990): 98.

[41] Ibid., 97.

[42] N.G. Kuznetsov, <u>Memoirs of Wartime Minister of the Navy</u> (Moscow: Progress Publishers, 1990), 53.

[43] Peter I. Gosztony, "The Spanish Civil War and Soviet Aid," <u>Military Review</u> 57 (January 1977): 27.

[44] Puzzo, 150-167.

[45] Willard C. Frank, "Multinational Naval Cooperation and the Spanish Civil War, 1936," <u>Naval War College Review</u> 47 (Spring 1994): 72.

[46] Ibid., 74.

[47] Edwards, 239.

[48] Frank, "Multinational Naval Cooperation and the Spanish Civil War, 1936," 77.

[49] Edwards, 233.

[50] Frank, "Multinational Naval Cooperation and the Spanish Civil War, 1936," 78.

[51] Ibid., 79-83.

[52] Ibid., 79-83.

[53] Edwards, 239.

[54] Ibid., 241.

[55] Frank, "Multinational Naval Cooperation and the Spanish Civil War, 1936," 91-92.

[56] Ibid., 92-96.

[57] Tanner, 131-133.

[58] Puzzo, 64.

[59] Tanner, 52.

[60] Ibid., 64-76.

[61] Ibid., 88-92.

[62] Ibid., 88-92.

[63] Ibid., 96.

[64] Ibid., 97.

[65] Ibid., 136.

[66] Ibid., 139.

[67] Ibid., 146.

[68] Ibid., 151.

[69] Ibid., 155-159.

[70] Louis Fischer, "Pirates and British Policy," The Nation, no. 145 (September 18, 1937): 282.

[71] Puzzo, 195-196.

[72] Peter Gretton, "The Nyon Conference – The Naval Aspect," The English Historical Review (January 1975): 104.

[73] Pratt, 88-93.

[74] Gretton, 107.

[75] Pratt, 91.

[76] Gretton, 109.

[77] Ibid., 111-112.

[78] Gosztony, 28.

[79] David T. Cattel, Communism and the Spanish Civil War (Berkeley, CA: University of California Press, 1956), 105.

[80] Ibid., 105.

[81] Robert W. Herrick, Soviet Naval Strategy: Fifty Years of Theory and Practice (Annapolis, MD: Naval Institute Publishers, 1968), 13-27.

[82] Willard C. Frank, "Naval Operations in the Spanish Civil War, 1936-1939," Naval War College Review 37 (January – February 1984): 32.

[83] Cattel, 104.

[84] Kuznetsov, 59.

[85] Frank, "Naval Operations in the Spanish Civil War, 1936-1939," 31.

[86] Ibid., 31.

[87] Kuznetsov, 61.

[88] Frank, "Naval Operations in the Spanish Civil War, 1936-1939," 46.

[89] Ibid., 35.

[90] Willard C. Frank, "Misperception and Incidents at Sea: The Deutschland and Leipzig Crises, 1937," Naval War College Review 43 (Spring 1990): 34.

[91] Ibid.,39-42.

[92] Kuznetsov, 33.

[93] Frank, 37.

[94] Herrick, 25.

[95] Kuznetsov, 64.

[96] Herrick, 34-35.

[97] Ibid., 27.

[98] Kuznetsov, 72.

[99] Sullivan, 718.

[100] Frank, "Naval Operations in the Spanish Civil War, 1936-1939," 49.

[101] Kuznetsov, 69.

[102] Patrick Abbazia, Mr. Roosevelt's Navy (Annapolis, MD: Naval Institute Press, 1975), 33-34.

[103] Kuznetsov, 71.

[104] Frank, "Multinational Naval Cooperation and the Spanish Civil War, 1936," 96.

[105] Frank, "Naval Operations in the Spanish Civil War, 1936-1939," 47.

[106] Jacob W. Kipp, The Spanish Civil War and the Politics of Future War: The Red Army's Assessment of War Experience and the Fate of the Theory of Deep Operations (Fort Leavenworth: Soviet Army Studies Office, U.S. Army Combined Arms Command, 1990), 3-12.

[107] Herrick, 43.

BIBLIOGRAPHY

Abbazia, Patrick. <u>Mr. Roosevelt's Navy</u>. Annapolis: Naval Institute Press, 1975.

Beevor, Anthony. <u>The Spanish Civil War</u>. New York: Peter Bedrick Books, 1983.

Cattel, David T. <u>Communism and the Spanish Civil War</u>. Berkeley: University of California Press, 1956.

Coverdale, John F. <u>Italian Intervention in the Spanish Civil War</u>. Princeton: Princeton University Press, 1975.

Edwards, Kenneth. <u>The Grey Diplomatists</u>. London: Rich and Cowan, Ltd., 1938.

Elstob, Peter. <u>Condor Legion</u>. New York: Ballantine Books, 1973.

Fischer, Louis. "Pirates and British Policy." <u>The Nation</u>, no. 145 (September 18, 1937): 282.

Frank, Willard C., Jr. "Misperception and Incidents at Sea: The Deutschland and Leipzig Crises, 1937." <u>Naval War College Review</u> 43 (Spring 1990): 31-46.

_____. "Multinational Naval Cooperation and the Spanish Civil War, 1936." <u>Naval War College Review</u> 47 (Spring 1994): 72-101.

_____. "Naval Operations in the Spanish Civil War, 1936-1939." <u>Naval War College Review</u> 37 (January – February 1984): 24-55.

_____. "Politico-Military Deception at Sea in the Spanish Civil War, 1936-1939." <u>Intelligence and National Security</u> 5 (July 1990): 84-112.

Gosztony, Peter I. "The Spanish Civil War and Soviet Aid." <u>Military Review</u>, 57 (January 1977): 26-33.

Gretton, Peter. "The Nyon Conference – The Naval Aspect." <u>The English Historical Review</u> (January 1975): 103-112.

Guttmann, Allen. <u>Problems in American Civilization</u>. Boston: DC Heath and Company, 1963.

Herrick, Robert W. <u>Soviet Naval Strategy: Fifty Years of Theory and Practice</u>. Annapolis: Naval Institute Publishers, 1968.

Kipp, Jacob W. The Spanish Civil War and the Politics of Future War: The Red Army's Assessment of War Experience and the Fate of the Theory of Deep Operations. Fort Leavenworth: Soviet Army Studies Office, U.S. Army Combined Arms Command, 1990.

Kuznetsov, N.G. <u>Memoirs of Wartime Minister of the Navy</u>. Moscow: Progress Publishers, 1990.

Maisky, Ivan. <u>Spanish Notebooks</u>. London: Hutchinson of London, 1966.

Pratt, Lawrence W. East of Malta, West of Suez: Britain's Mediterranean Crisis, 1936-1939. Cambridge, England: Cambridge University Press, 1975.

Puzzo, Dante A. Spain and the Great Powers, 1936-1941. New York: Columbia University Press, 1962.

Roskill, Stephen W. Naval Policy Between the Wars: The Period of Reluctant Rearmament, 1930-1939. Annapolis: Naval Institute Press, 1976.

Sullivan, Brian R. "Fascist Italy's Military Involvement in the Spanish Civil War." Journal of Military History 59 (October 1995): 697-727.

Thomas, Hugh. The Spanish Civil War. New York: Harper & Row, 1977.

Tanner, Stephen William. German Naval Intervention in the Spanish Civil War as Reflected by the German Records. Washington, DC: The American University Library, 1976.

Whealey, Robert H. Hitler and Spain: the Nazi Role in the Spanish Civil War, 1936-1939. Lexington: University Press of Kentucky, 1989.

Young, Robert J. In Command of France: French Foreign Policy and Military Planning, 1933-1940. Cambridge, MA: Harvard University Press, 1978.